I MISSED MY MOLLY MORMON CERTIFICATE BY A STITCH

BY KIMBERLY OLSEN

ILLUSTRATIONS BY DUSTIN BAIRD

10 9 8 7 6 5 4 3 2 1

I MISSED MY
MOLLY MORMON
CERTIFICATE
BY A STITCH

THIS BOOK IS DEDICATED TO:

Charlene Manwaring (my mother) for teaching all I needed to be a Molly . . . Thanks, Mom.
Darwin Olsen, my husband, for enduring my teasing and taking it so well. I adore you.
And to my children: Allen, Cassie, Holly, Joseph, Laura-Leigh, and Darwin Olsen Jr. (affectionately called D.J.).
You have made me what I am. I love you all.

ACKNOWLEDGMENTS

A writer never works alone when preparing a manuscript and I am no different. I wish to pay tribute to those who helped me through this adventure. Thanks to Georgia Carpenter for seeing the potential of this book and publishing it and to Darla Isackson for her wonderful editing skills! This has been an exciting adventure! Thanks go to Jana Dibble who always believed I could do it. Also thanks to Kathy Behrend, my oldest friend in the world, for the laughter, the advice, and the persistent nudging, to Jo Anne Dickey for showing me the true character of Charity, to Bobi Moore for investing so much in my dreams. Thanks to Hal Manwaring (my dad) and Nicollette Parsons for the use of their typewriters. Aren't you glad I finally have my own? I could not have finished this without you all. Also, thanks to all the people who suffered through my endless explanations and dreams for this book.

And last, but in no way least, thanks to my husband, Darwin Olsen, who has suffered through nights of typing and never complained and has taken my teasing with grace and wit. Thank you all.

TABLE OF CONTENTS

INTRODUCTION

THERE IS A MYTH AMONG THE WOMEN OF THE CHURCH. I'm not sure how it got started, but it circulates around the world—infiltrating every ward, every family, and every woman's heart. Maybe it stemmed from our collective desire to become perfected (see Matthew 5:48), or maybe there actually was such a woman once; I don't know. Wherever the Myth came from, it is part of our lives and often affects the way we feel about ourselves and the way we look at others.

Who is this mythical person? Why Molly Mormon, of course. Molly Mormon—that paragon of virtue, brimming with skill in all the womanly arts, talent oozing from every pore, a heart as big as Texas and beauty to write sonnets about!

Molly Mormon is a cross between:

MARY POPPINS: Practically perfect in every way, down to the spoonful of sugar.

MOTHER TERESA: Untiring in compassionate service and humanitarian causes.

OLIVIA WALTON: Those in my generation know who she is—"Good night, John-Boy."

With a splash of:

RAQUEL WELCH: OK, so I can dream, can't I?

We've all heard of Molly, even feared her. I'll bet you could think of someone you consider a "Molly" this very minute. Which one of us hasn't sat in Relief Society and withered as "SHE" is praised and her virtues extolled? And what about homemaking meeting, my personal favorite for feeling inadequate? You see, I was not blessed with any talent in my hands (unless you count holding a pencil properly a talent). I have the gift of gab, not craftiness.

Female converts to the Church are spared a lifetime of practicing and auditioning for the role, but it doesn't stop them from trying to become like Molly after they join, sometimes even harder than those of us raised in the Church. We all want to be Molly, and we all fall short.

Through this little book, my sisters, I want to give you hope and say "relax!" All we can do is be the best "us" we can be. Then, maybe, we will see that in becoming our best, we can achieve a more real and enviable stature than the one so prized by LDS women today—Molly Mormondom! Don't forget, Molly is a myth; she is simply all of our best traits and talents compiled into one legendary but mythical being. We all contribute to her greatness!

Here are the most common Molly beliefs:

THE MOLLY CREED

1) We believe in sewing, painting, and all other handcrafts.

2) We believe that a woman will be judged on her own casserole and not for anyone else's.

3) We believe that through myriads of music lessons, all childrendom will be refined by practice and recitals.

4) We believe that the first principles of house cleaning are:
    1st: Faith that there's a house under all the clutter.
    2nd: Resourcefulness.
    3rd: Buying at D.I. for the relief of the pocketbook.
    4th: Laying on of hands for that sparkle on your floors and sinks.

5) We believe that a woman must be dressed in the latest Molly fashions by sewing and by shopping at thrift stores and yard sales.

6) We believe in the same organization that has existed for all time: namely; fathers, mothers, children, pets, plants, and so forth.

7) We believe in the gift of chivalrous, sensitive, caring, strong and sure husbands.

8) We believe the scriptures to be of great value as long as we can keep our husbands and children awake long enough to read them.

9) We believe in being subject to sales, coupons, discounts, and bargain basements, in maintaining, sustaining and stretching our cash flow.

10) We believe the gospel to be the truth and allow all our children the same privilege, let them murmur how, where, or when they may—they still have to go to church.

11) We claim the privilege of assigning chores to whomever we choose, without prior notice, and without input.

12) We believe in the literal gathering of the Vulture Club and in the disappearance of all

✖

the goodies in the house; that Moms have a right to get perturbed; that Dads don't have a clue; and that the kids won't know why until they are parents.

13) We believe in being honest, true, chaste, benevolent, virtuous and in doing good to all people; Indeed we may say that we follow the admonition of Molly—we believe in compassionate service and in taking bread to all our neighbors. If there is anything virtuous, lovely, or of good taste, we seek after these things!

CRAFTY HOMEMAKING

FIRST OF ALL, I'D LIKE TO THANK MY MOM for all the countless hours she spent in trying to teach me the feminine arts that would assure I become a Molly. Not that it did much good, but "Thanks, Mom!" I swear my mother was from the Golden Days of Yore. She had four daughters and she insisted we suffer through years of training in the feminine arts. I'm sure Mom is the closest anyone ever came to being a real Molly.

She can do everything! She is a professional seamstress and makes clothes to sell. She makes the best dolls in town and can make a gorgeous quilt from old denim squares she cuts from used jeans. Because she was a dedicated mother, she tried to teach her daughters those same skills. She even had a prophet to back up her words and efforts in this regard, because Brigham Young said:

> "I believe in indulging children, in a reasonable way. If the girls want dolls, shall they have them? Yes. But must they be taken to the dressmakers to be dressed? No. Let the girls learn to cut and sew the clothing for their dolls, and in a few years they will know how to make a dress for themselves and others."
>
> (*Discourses of Brigham Young*, p. 210)

I was not impressed. In fact, sewing gives me hives! When I even think about sewing, my hands shake, I get all sweaty, and I can't breathe. My aversion to sewing and all other handcrafts comes partly from being dyslexic! I can see a project in my mind and it looks beautiful until I start doing it. My husband even hates me to cut bread. I never cut it straight. That also goes for patterns, cheese, roast, etc. I've just learned to ask someone else to do the cutting.

Consequently, I have been very happy to see sewing go the way of all the world. I hated sewing when I was a child, and I still hate it. I was rescued from it by a simple economic reality: today it's cheaper to buy clothes at thrift stores than it is to make them. I love thrift stores. Nothing makes me feel better than getting a quality item for a great price. Sometimes I've even found new clothes with the tags on, and the price I pay for them is a fraction of their original cost.

My kids love going to D.I., and when I take them we end up spending more time than money. You'd think I'd taken them to Disneyland—and with the cost of travel these days, D.I. is as close as they'll ever get to that amusement park.

My mom could draw and paint, too, and she wanted her daughters to find the joys of creating something beautiful with their hands. I couldn't do that, either. All I got for my efforts was frustration. So I've stayed away from these things that give me stress. This poses a problem because homemaking meeting offers classes every month in ways to improve your skills in crafts. My greatest fear is that someday I'll have to serve as homemaking counselor. The only reason I'm even invited back to homemaking meeting now is for comic relief. I don't even sign up for a project anymore and no one asks me to.

Once we received a survey in Relief Society on what would interest us to do in homemaking meetings in the coming year. They sent that out just for me—I know it. On the other hand, I love to go and listen to the lesson and sample the tasty food. I do get asked to bring things to eat quite frequently, but the craft part of the night becomes a stress.

I try to cover up by cracking jokes and making everyone forget that I'm not doing anything. I've got it down to a science. I'm never in one place too long and I dazzle people with my charm and wit and my keen sense of color and style. Remember that I can see something in my mind but it gets all jumbled by the time it gets to my hands. They have done some projects that I thought I would like so much that I broke down and purchased the kit. As you might guess, I have boxes in my garage that store my unfinished projects.

I did find that I could arrange flowers! I love to do that and not long ago I signed up for the flower arranging class and finished one arrangement and started another before I went home. My friends at Relief Society, my husband, and my mother were all shocked. I wasn't, because I have always loved to do that sort of thing. I remember as a little girl picking beautiful flowers such as dandelions, clover, and morning glory. I would bring them into the house and put them in glasses, arranging them just right, and setting them in the middle of the dining room table. Mom told me they were weeds but I didn't care; they were beautiful to me.

I was thrilled to learn that my own children liked the same type of "flowers," and I have had several glasses filled with them all summer long. I didn't have the heart to tell my kids they were considered weeds. I'd let them learn that at school. My son even renamed dandelions. He called them "dandyflowers." I love that name and all of my children call them dandyflowers, too. It's under protest that I kill them in the spring. I think the yard looks pretty covered in yellow, but my neighbor doesn't want them in his, so I have to spray for them. When I have control over my own world, dandyflowers will be as precious as roses. Can't you just hear Juliet saying, "A dandyflower by any other name is still a dandyflower?" I can.

I like to make my house look as good as possible. I love the crafty look and have been very glad that you can go right downtown and buy handmade crafts—at least you can in my neck of the woods. My friends also make things and give them to me, so I have lots of handmade items and only those closest to me know I took no part in their creation.

My girls have inherited my mother's talents and now I'm buying craft kits for them. They are good at crafts and ever so often they'll want to teach me how to do one. Before long they remember why I don't do that sort of thing, and they won't ask me again for awhile.

For a long time I thought I was alone in my quest to hide my dislike for doing crafts, but one night at homemaking I bumped into someone else trying to hide her inadequacies and we had a great laugh. It soon dawned on me that there's a whole group of women who don't particularly like that sort of thing, and we've formed a support group. We often meet the night after homemaking meeting and it's a comfort to us all! I have learned I'm not the only woman with boxes full of unfinished projects hiding in the garage. It's also a comfort to remember that making crafts is not a prerequisite to the Celestial Kingdom. I might make it after all.

TURN THE NUKE-BOX ON

MOM ALWAYS SAID, "THE WAY TO A MAN'S HEART IS THROUGH HIS STOMACH." She was right! My husband fondly tells the story of his parent's first meal together. His mother prepared the meal on a woodburning cookstove (now that's slaving over a hot stove!) for his father while they were courting (old-fashioned word for dating). Isn't that romantic? You can bet she knew the old adage about men's hearts and stomachs. I really want to learn to cook on one of those stoves. It might add some "spark" to my marriage!

Even today, a home-cooked meal will make a man's heart flutter. In the age of fast foods, a man will swoon at the smell of home cooking; mine always does, though it could be from shock that I've actually cooked for a change. My husband fell in love with me over a hot loaf of bread I had just taken from the oven. I might have failed craft training but I passed cooking with flying colors! Cooking is where I get my relaxation. I find it downright comforting, whenever I can spare the time.

Because she had four daughters and was from the Golden Days of Yore, Mom took her job of teaching us to be good wives and mothers seriously. I was ten when my cooking education began. First lesson—how to make bread. It was wonderful! I soon found myself at the head of my class.

Now remember, this was the early '70s and we didn't have fancy machines to help mix, knead, or bake the bread. I learned how to make bread the old-fashioned way, messy hands and all. There's nothing like feeling that sticky dough squish between your fingers or kneading the dough for ten minutes. I know that's why the pioneer women didn't need psychiatrists. They punched the snot out of the bread dough and got out all their frustrations. Who needs a shrink when there's bread dough to knead!

It didn't take me long to realize that cooking was shrouded in mystery and folklore. After Mom had finished kneading the dough, she poked a hole right in the middle, then draped a towel lovingly over it.

"Why did you poke a hole in the dough?" I asked.

"I don't know. My mother always did, so I do."

When I asked Grandma, I got the same answer—her mother did, so she did. As far as I know, there is no real reason why rising dough gets a belly button. It probably started way back when Eve was making bread. Maybe she got bored and for variety poked a hole in the middle of one batch. The idea caught on and the next thing you know, women in the latter days are carrying on the time-honored tradition. If anyone knows the scientific reason, please tell me.

I mastered bread, cookies, cake, and pie. You name it, I could bake it. Success at baking made me feel better about myself considering the fact that I failed so miserably at crafts and sewing. Of course, not everything I made turned out perfectly; I did have moments of disappointment. My first pie brings back some memories. The filling was extraordinary. Too bad no one ever got to taste it. I made the piecrust from scratch, exactly the way Mom showed me.

She never used a recipe; her mind was a veritable recipe box. Put in a pinch of this and a dash of that and Presto—perfection! So, following her example, I began my infamous pie. I put flour, salt, baking powder, shortening, and water in a bowl. Then I mixed it, rolled it, filled it and baked it. After it cooled we tried to cut it—but a jackhammer couldn't have cut it!

"What did you do to this piecrust?" Mom asked.

"Nothing! I did it just like you do—flour, salt, baking powder, shortening, and water," I replied defensively.

"There is no baking powder in pie crust," Mom giggled. I thought she was going to die laughing. I was not amused.

"Oh," I said.

Later, I actually came across a piecrust recipe that included baking powder, but it also called for eggs and vinegar—probably to make it cuttable.

After the first disaster my pies got better. I became so good at piecrust that my friends would ask me to make theirs. I struck up a deal with them: crusts for crafts. That's fair enough, wouldn't you say?

It didn't take long to figure out why Mom was teaching us how to cook. As soon as we got proficient at it, she quit! The kitchen was ours and she could have a life. By the time I was sixteen, I could cook an entire Thanksgiving dinner, which is exactly what I did, homemade stuffing and all.

Because I had to do so much of it, I soon lost my excitement about cooking. Boys and school and all the things teenagers do seemed more fulfilling than kitchen duties. Thank goodness, I had two younger sisters. They'd get their turn in the kitchen, and I'd be free. But for all my complaining, when it came time for me to run the kitchen, I could do it. I was ready and able when a lot of my friends were still wondering how. There was a method to Mom's madness; it wasn't just laziness!

After I was married I spent hours in the kitchen creating masterpieces of culinary delight. My husband thought he had hit the jackpot. He didn't even mind sewing on all those buttons and doing hems because he was so richly rewarded in the kitchen.

That was then; this is now. With the pace of the world today, even at our house, cooking is becoming a lost art. I was a relic for years, refusing to conform to "new-wave" cooking. I hate to admit that I used to look down my nose at moms who used a microwave. Didn't they know that cooking for their family was not a race? OK, so I was stupid, but poverty kept the old ways in our home for a long time—we couldn't afford a microwave. But finally one of our friends bought a new one and handed the old one down to us. As soon as I had a microwave and learned how wonderful it was, I changed my tune.

I have joined the ranks of microwave families, often "nuking" my children's food and feeling thankful for the technology. With three teenagers and three more coming up I now have no time to spend in the kitchen. I've tried to teach my girls to take over, but they resist—kinda like I did with sewing. Two of my boys like to cook so I'm not giving up hope yet, but everyone is so busy with basketball, soccer, Mutual, missionary work and PTA that food preparation isn't even on our list. So I now love my nuke-box and I sincerely apologize to any of you who might have been offended by my haughty attitude before I became initiated.

I also got a bread maker, and Mom almost hyperventilated.

"Bread made in those machines just doesn't taste as good," she says. I beg to differ. I love starting bread with singleness of heart before I go to church and having a fresh loaf ready to eat by the time we get home. Of course, there are still times I make bread the old way, especially when I have a need to punch someone out. Kneading bread dough is still good for that.

One thing I've learned is that the LDS people have their own unique ways of cooking. It's partly due to the Word of Wisdom and partly due to tradition. Being raised most of my life in the "Heart of

Zion" (Idaho), where almost everyone I knew was LDS, I saw nothing peculiar about us. Our way of life was THE way of life. Then we moved to Portland, Oregon. Life in the big city was different, to say the least. I learned that as a people, we *are* peculiar.

I got the opportunity to do some baking for a friend who owned a small canteen. I had been baking for twenty years and felt confident in my ability to please even the most picky palate. I lost all confidence when my non-Mormon friend came back with at least a dozen complaints about my oatmeal cookies. Did you know that the world doesn't put cinnamon in their oatmeal cookies? I couldn't believe it! I have always put spice in oatmeal cookies. It enhances the raisins. After several days of complaints, my friend wanted to know what cookbook I was using. "Why, 10th and 19th Ward's, of course."

"Ah! Mormon cookies," she said, and went right home and copied her worldly recipes. Handing them to me she said "Use these and see how they work."

It took about a month, but I finally perfected "In the World" cookies. I'm now set to please any group, Mormon or Non. However, in the last few years I've noticed that the stores have begun to offer Mormon cookbooks for the general public to buy. I can just hear those Gentiles now: "Here's a new and exotic dish, Tuna Casserole. I found it in that new Mormon cookbook."

Casseroles! What a concept. I'm sure they were invented by an LDS mother with eight hungry kids to feed and only 1/2 a pound of hamburger to work with. Add some celery, onion, stewed tomatoes, (from last year's garden) and a can of zesty tomato soup, boil some noodles, mix with the meat sauce, top with grated cheese and you've got a meal fit for a king! It'll feed twelve and most of the ingredients were from your food storage!

Soups are another LDS specialty. Go into any Latter-day Saint home and somewhere, probably sitting in a place of honor, there will be a soup pot big enough for a two-year-old to sit in—all of mine did whenever it wasn't full of soup! My husband is still amazed at the fact that I can take what's left of a turkey after the Vulture Club is finished with it and make enough soup to feed the entire U.S. Navy. Can't everyone? He even tells people I put everything but the kitchen sink in my soups. Well, the fridge has to be cleaned out sometimes, and I've found porcelain and aluminum don't make good soup stock.

As we near the end of the century and are on the brink of Star Trek technology, I'm grateful for the inventions that have made preparing meals easier and faster. I certainly can't spend all day in the kitchen anymore, and I don't know anyone else who can, either. I love to cook and I will teach my kids the old ways, just in case they are ever needed again. But for now it's so much easier to tell the kids to turn on the nuke-box and prepare dinner.

NONE OF MY KIDS PLAY THE PIANO

MUSIC LESSONS! THE THOUGHT SENDS SHIVERS DOWN MY SPINE. Which one of us hasn't suffered through them in our quest for Molly Mormondom? Right from the very beginning, my childhood was filled with them. My siblings and I had lots of music training. Our Medieval Mother said our education would not be complete without music. There was always a piano standing majestically in a special corner of the living room. It was one of Mom's prized possessions. What a beautiful instrument, capable of such Celestial sounds—except when my fingers touched the keys!

For some reason I've never been able to get my fingers, eyes, and feet to work together with my brain—and that's what it takes to play the piano. It's not that I don't know the theory; I had six years of music theory. I know the notes, I know where they are on the keyboard, I even know how they sound—I just can't get the piano part right. I've tried, but to play the piano you have to:

1) SIT: Which is hard for me. (I've been told I'm hyper.)

2) PRACTICE: It might make perfect, but I always wanted to sing and dance and think of boys, instead.

3) HAVE TALENT: I have talent, just not in my hands—remember dyslexia?

So, Mom gave up and I got voice lessons, instead. I did better at singing. Since my first solo when I was four, I knew that interacting with an audience was for me. I had been asked to sing "I Wonder When He Comes Again" at the dedication of the new church building our ward had just completed. The song was new, my dress was new and I even got to hold a microphone. I still remember the time

I spent learning the song and the excitement of donning my pink dress with the white collar and standing in front of a full chapel. I was too young to be frightened, so I thoroughly enjoyed it! I knew then that the limelight was for me. There was no way I was gonna sit behind a piano when I could be right out front stealing the show. My sister plays beautifully, so piano perfection pressure was taken from me and I was free to love singing.

Mom would gather us around the piano (she could play) and we would learn to sing hymns, in parts. Later, when I became a teenager I decided it was a drag—all that singing and familial bliss, but now those are some of my most comforting memories. I learned all the hymns and could find them in the book without consulting the index. It really threw me for a loop when they changed the page numbers and keys in the hymnbooks. I was lost for months.

My mom was the Primary chorister all my childhood and so we learned all the Primary songs, too. We practiced so much we were pretty good and began to get invitations to perform in other wards. So we took our act on the road and I think we would have made it big if those Osmonds hadn't beaten us to it.

I began waving my arm for Primary when I was sixteen, and have done so off and on ever since. I say "waving my arm" because, for all my music training, I must have been absent the day they taught about leading because I honestly didn't know there was any kind of method to it—until I had a husband to point it out to me. I had just been called to lead the music in Primary and he was the Blazer leader. Even though he knew the limitations of my talents in music, he was totally shocked as he watched me lead the first time. He's a musician in his own right and so he sweetly explained the correct method of music leading.

Oh no! I was expected to sing, wave my arm, and count out the beats—all while listening to the children? I had given up the piano because of lack of coordination, and now I was expected to have it? I never quite grasped the concept during that stint of being Primary chorister. I was too nervous. No one ever complained, though, because I knew all the songs and my voice carried the kids through if they forgot the words. No one complained; no one, that is, except my husband.

Sometimes, I'd be waving my arm and those kids would be singing like angels and I'd look back at my husband and he'd be counting out the beats for me—down, over, up—down, over, up. Well I'd get so flustered I'd forget the words, my name, and even how to wave. It was a trial for both of us, to say the least. I did not want to learn how to lead music from my husband—a pride thing, I guess.

Did I ever learn to direct music correctly and did my husband and I ever resolve the waving of the arm issue? Of course, but not by my own choice. I was happy and secure just waving my arm. The children didn't know the difference and my husband got a new calling, so I was content.

But there's one thing I've learned about the Church—once you get content in a calling, you usually get a new one! Since we know inspiration is involved in the decisions made by the bishop, I've come to learn that Heavenly Father has quite a sense of humor. He also must hate to see issues go unresolved between spouses, because when I least expected it, I was called to be ward choir director. I wanted to faint and I did laugh right out loud. I thought my husband was going to get a bloody tongue, he was biting it so hard. The bishop's counselor wasn't sure how to take us.

"You've got to be kidding! Right?" I asked. I could hear my husband trying to control a snort. I shot him a dirty look.

"No. You've done so well with the Primary we feel you're just what the ward choir needs," he said innocently.

Again I looked at my husband, whose face was as red as his hair and he just smiled. I wanted to stomp on his toe.

"I was faking it!" I blurted, frantically. "I can't lead music! Ask *him*!" I pointed to my husband who looked wide-eyed at the counselor but remained silent. I wanted to scream.

"Those kids sure sing wonderfully. You'll do just fine."

In a moment of rebellion I accepted the call. I was not going to let my husband think I was chicken. Rebellion lasted about thirty seconds after we left the bishop's office. How could I lead a group of adults most of whom knew more about music than I did? Desperation forced me to accept help from my husband which he gave quite gallantly.

It took about four months to learn to lead music the right way, and I didn't learn, in the privacy of my own home. I started my first choir practice totally unable to lead correctly. Thank goodness, everyone was patient with me and the accompanist had a sense of humor. She could lead music and gave me a crash course in leading. Everyone in the choir joined in. We laughed a lot and yes, my husband was in the choir, lovingly beating time in the tenor section. Sometimes the entire choir would be helping me beat time.

All in all, I learned to lead music properly and the issue between my husband and me is resolved. We even laugh about it now. When I stand to lead he can watch me without having a coronary, and I can do it without wanting to kick him. The best part is, I can do it! I don't expect to be guest conductor for the Tabernacle Choir, but I can do it! I hope Heavenly Father is happy, because I am, and so is my husband.

Did any of my six kids get any musical talent? Right now we're averaging about half and half. My oldest son is brimming with talent and has stage presence. He can sing with perfect pitch and he's first chair in the trombone section. He's now learning to play the drums. I'm quite proud of him.

Two of my daughters sing . . . constantly . . . in monotone! I thought for a while that my oldest child got all the talent and there was none left for anyone else. It made me sad and the singing drove me crazy. My girls love to sing and they should. I don't think it's good for their self-esteem to tell them they can't, so I suffer in silence. I have taken them to the piano and made them listen to the way the song should sound. Granted, my piano needs to be tuned, but it sounds better than they do. (Sorry girls).

I do have one daughter with a voice. One out of three isn't bad. She's proved to be quite good on the flute, too, and more recently the piano. She's a natural.

That leaves two boys. My eleven-year-old has a wonderful voice but refuses to sing in public. He's plagued with stage fright, though I'm not sure how that happened. I live to perform and he clams up. Lately he's noticed that the girls go all goo-goo eyed when he sings and suddenly girls are important to him, so maybe they can achieve what I've failed to do. My seven-year-old is showing potential, although he likes sports better than music. He can belt out Primary songs, though, so I'm hopeful.

I haven't forced my kids to play the piano, but when they want to learn, I arrange music lessons for them. I do make them sing around the piano, though. Music lives on in our home and I'm even taking the time to sit and practice the piano, myself. I'm no Marvin Goldstein but now that dancing and boys are no longer my main priorities, I can concentrate when I practice. I'm certainly not where I want to be and I have a way to go before I'd dare play in public, but I might be ready to play in church . . . during the Millennium.

Even My Silk Plants Die

ONE OF MY MAJOR CHARACTER FLAWS IS THAT I CAN'T STAND CLUTTER. It makes me crazy! So, of course, I have been blessed with a house full of slobs! You know the type—they can't see the pile of toys on the floor, (even after plowing through them fifty times), but will dog-pile on a single dollar bill.

I've heard that "cleanliness is next to godliness." It stands to reason, then, that because children have recently arrived from the premortal world, they'd at least have a latent tendency to be neat. Don't I wish! When they pass through the veil, they truly forget everything!

I have been trying for almost seventeen years to teach my children to clean up after themselves. I guess I'm doing something wrong. I know they're smart, I know they think, but out of six kids only one will voluntarily help me. He just turned seven. I give him six more months, tops, and he'll join the others. There's nothing like the look on a teenager's face as you lecture them about sanitation regulations and fines for toxic waste in their bedrooms. Some of the best mold cultures I've ever found have come from under their beds.

It is not for my health that I stand my children around a bed and try to teach them, for the millionth time, how to do hospital corners and clean the junk from underneath. I just don't want their mission companions to think they are slobs!

Like most women in the church, a lot of my self-esteem comes from the condition of my house. I haven't got much esteem left! I'm a good housekeeper—I know I am—but you'd never tell it by my house. It never looks the way I want it to. My family thinks I'm a lunatic. They don't see anything wrong with the way things look. They're too busy trying to win at a computer game or find "Gilligan's Island" on cable TV.

I have become content (ha) to have my house clean once a week, for a few hours. The rest of the week I putter around trying to redo what has been undone by myriads of small and not-so-small hands. We play a fun game at our house. Maybe you play it, too—it's called "Round Robin." These are the rules: Mom starts to clean in one room while everyone is in another. As soon as she's done, everyone congregates in the clean room and messes it up, so that by the time she's cleaned through the house, it's time to start over.

President Brigham Young said:

> "A good housewife, whether she possesses much or little, will have a place for every thing she has in the house and her home orderly and comfortable, and everything when wanted can be found in its place."
>
> *(Discourses of Brigham Young*, p. 213)

I would be the happiest mom in town if I could convince my family that this is Doctrine. The only things in my house that I can find are my things—if, of course, someone hasn't moved them.

Of course it makes it harder for the children to grasp the concept of everything in its place when Dad uses the living room as a closet. I'm always tripping over his shoes and sitting on his coat. His hats make attractive dining room chair decor. I finally replaced the chairs with benches and now we can never find Daddy's hat.

If I did counted cross stitch, I'd make a sampler of the scripture:

> "Behold mine house is a house of order, saith the Lord God, and not a house of confusion." (D&C 132:8)

Maybe my family would get the hint.

In decorating my house I have gone with the early D.I. theme. It's only been in the last year that I finally got matching furniture. Before, I told everyone that having nothing matching except for the furniture covers was a fashion statement. No one got to see the covers anyway, with all the coats and piles of clean laundry dumped on them. I don't even remember what color the carpet is, but who cares? The toys are happy, which makes the kids happy, which should make me happy, but it doesn't.

My piano graces the living room with its beauty and you can't even see the peanut butter and jelly smeared on the legs and sides unless you look really close. My walls are covered with fingerprints and an extensive art collection. Anyone who walks into my house knows what religion I practice just by the pictures on the walls. The wall to wall kids are a good clue, too.

I was impressed as I walked through the Idaho Falls Temple once and saw a woman dusting the silk plants. There's never a speck of dust in the temple. Many people work to keep it spotless—and rightly so. My problem is there's only me really trying to keep our house clean. My silk plants are in sad shape. I never remember to dust them. They usually die of suffocation.

My greatest fear is that the Millennium will be ushered in and my house will be a disaster. I hope I'll be able to sit at the Savior's feet and listen to His words instead of rushing around shoveling toys, clothes, and hats out of the way. Which brings me to an all-important question for all those moms out there who are like me: Are you a Mary or a Martha? (Read Luke 10:38-42). Which am I? At this point I'm a Martha for sure, which is why I say my dislike for clutter is a character flaw. My house is clean, just cluttered. I'm not admitting anything about the garage. My kids don't have to worry about catching any horrible diseases, and my husband is quite happy, so maybe I should just relax! And I will, right after I straighten those furniture covers!

I'M SURE MY SPIRIT IS SKINNY

If I had been born in the Renaissance Period my figure would be a classic. Now? I'm just round. It's not that I'm grossly obese; I just don't wear the size three I did in high school. But that was B.C. (Before Children).

As a teenager, I was vain—just ask my mother. She would say that someday I would get my "come-upance"—whatever that meant. Of course, I didn't believe it until I looked at my swollen body, streaked with stretch marks as I waited for the birth of my first child. The words of my mother came back to haunt me. I promptly had a good cry with my old friend, Vanity. Now, after giving birth to five children (I have a stepdaughter who didn't contribute to the size of my clothes), I have had to re-evaluate my relationship with Vanity.

I know I'll never be a stick again and I doubt I'd be happy if I were, but I certainly would be willing to find out. Let's face it, I'm a woman now, not a girl. It was a shock when my Mom told me that, but I've adjusted to it. It's still a jolt when I look in the mirror—my mind feels eighteen but I look thirty-something!

Since I became a mother, I have attained an even more sure testimony that Heavenly Father has a sense of humor. First, my body is shaped—well, it's just too funny to describe. My hands, wrists and ankles are the only places not affected by childbearing. Every other place has added inches I didn't have before. It's been a challenge for me, considering I'm such good friends with Vanity. My dad just smiles and says I'm built just like my grandmother. Well, that's just great, except I'm not a grandmother yet! A wise friend once told me my matronly shape was beautiful because it was a testimony of my motherhood. Works for me!

I really worked hard for this figure, but I must admit, it would be nice to have a model's figure, just for awhile.

It makes me crazy to watch commercials or see ads for—well, anything. Apparently, if you're not 5'10" and a size one or two, you are not considered beautiful enough to be a model. I'm happy I finally reached 5 feet even, and not even my ring size is a one or two. However, my husband thinks I'm beautiful, and since he's one of the most honest people I know, I believe him! Anyway, I'd look ridiculous in the worldly fashions those models tout. I'm glad we LDS women have our own fashions; they are much more becoming on my figure and I have the same figure type as a lot of other girls—ooops, women. Besides, those TV models are cloned, you know, like on Star Trek? No one could be that skinny or perfect in real life—could they?

President Brigham Young said:

> "Let the sisters take care of themselves, and make themselves beautiful, and if any of you are so superstitious and ignorant as to say that this is pride, I can say that you are not informed as to the pride which is sinful before the Lord, you are also ignorant as to the excellency of the heavens, and of the beauty which dwells in the society of the Gods. Were you to see an angel, you would see a beautiful and lovely creature. Make yourselves like the angels in goodness and beauty."
>
> (*Discourses*, p. 215)

I love Brigham Young quotes, don't you? When I found this quote I showed it to my mother. It's hard to argue with a prophet. Sometimes, even my husband teases me about being in my "vain mode," just because I don't like to kiss him right after I get my lipstick on and if anyone touches my hair after it's finished I have a coronary. I haven't got much to work with so I have to guard what I do have.

I used to be proud of my almost flawless skin, but as I get older, I'm getting acne, which I never had as a teenager. My nails and hair grow really fast, but my hair is being invaded with grey. My teeth are perfectly straight, without braces. I'm not bragging, I'm just reminding myself that I do have some good attributes. It's a comfort to know that I am a child of God and that He likes variety, and that beauty is within, not without.

Sounds great, huh? It's the speech I give myself every time I look in the mirror and die of shock; my eighteen-year-old mind can't fathom the realities of my thirty-something body!

I REFUSE TO CUT THE APRON STRINGS

MOTHERHOOD . . . THE CROWN OF WOMAN . . . A SACRED TRUST . . . AN HONOR! Every girl in the Church is told this from the beginning of her life. It's part of the Molly Creed, and it's true; but nobody said Truth was easy—at least no one I know. The further I get into this Mother thing, the harder it gets.

Let's start right at the very beginning of motherhood. Do you remember when you were expecting your first baby? All the excitement, all the joy, all the happiness! It lasts clear until you get a different perspective of the toilet! I became well acquainted with Mr. Tidy-Bowl every single time I had a baby. He became my best friend for a while. I hardly gained any weight during the Tidy-Bowl part of pregnancy, but when the sickness ended the pounds stacked on! I had never seen anyone else blow up like a balloon, but I did it five times! Vanity was horrified at all the stretch marks and fatness, and so was I. Of course, Vanity got used to the stretch marks and they eventually became a symbol of honor.

My first childbirth experience brought me to the brink of death. Had I been a pioneer woman, I would have died, but thanks to modern technology, I have a scar down my belly five inches long. It offsets the stretch marks. Waking from surgery, I remember my husband's smiling face.

"We have a son!" He said beaming.

"Oh good." I said and drifted back to sleep.

When I finally got a good look at my son, I was shocked! He was premature and newborn and, well . . . have you ever seen a spider monkey? That's what they handed me—a spider monkey. I looked at the nurse and said:

"Take this one back and get me a cute one. I almost died for this kid and I deserve a cute one."

Everyone insisted he was mine, so I tried to get used to the idea and go on with life.

"He'll get cuter, I promise." Mom said.

"I hope so." I replied, doubtfully.

It took four days to figure out a name for my little spider monkey. Curious George was my first choice, but no. Still, they told me I couldn't take the baby home until I gave it a name. I think they were afraid he'd never be named if I didn't do it there. So I bought a book of names and began to search. This kid needed a fighting chance. He needed a name to help him through his little monkey life so I started with the A's: Aaron . . . Adam . . . . Allen. Allen means handsome. ALLEN—HANDSOME; Allen it was! On to the B's. Bartholomew . . . Benjamin . . . Brock. Brock means Masculine or Badger. BROCK—MASCULINE. Yes!

Thus my tiny, hair-covered spider monkey was given the name Allen Brock, meaning handsome masculine fighter. I am happy to report that he has lived up to his name and is a wonderful-looking young man. After I learned that most newborn babies are not beauty contest winners, I was able to look at them and say how truly beautiful they really are.

There's more to being a mother than just having babies. Those cute, sweet bundles of joy grow up; it's a sad thing, but true. Those wonderful innocent infants become destructo-maniacs called toddlers. To a toddler, nothing is safe or sacred. I know we get our children when they are tiny harmless babies so that by the time they are terrible we love them too much to do anything too drastic. Aren't they cute when they're learning to walk? They're cute until you're chasing them down the street in your nightgown . . . or trying to reach them before they destroy the cake you were about to take to your new neighbors!

Then, too, parents spend every day after the birth of their child trying to get them to say something. First words are an event to celebrate . . . for about five seconds; as soon as children learn to articulate, they never shut up!

I'm particularly fond of four-year-olds. Free agency is their middle name. They are quite eager to try out this new-found concept. Although it's a true principle, I'm not sure it should be put in the sticky hands of a four-year-old. No matter what, they will not do what you ask.

Only eight outdoes four. By then, they know everything and are eager to share their knowledge with their parents—usually something like this: "But Mawm! Pink does go with green, see?"

You're happy to get them baptized, just in case they don't live to be nine! Then all of a sudden they mellow out long enough to give you hope, before adolescence strikes! I'm totally confused on the issue of adolescence. I remember what it felt like to be a teenager but they keep telling me things have changed! I know it's been a few years, but I doubt human nature has changed since I was growing up.

Fortunately, my teenagers are pretty good. I don't worry too much, except about the daughter who is exactly like I was. She worries me because I remember. My mom just smiles and reminds me that she cursed me with five kids like me and so far I've got at least two.

My oldest son—remember the spider monkey?—wanted to drive more than anything. He took Driver's Ed., got his license and then couldn't drive because his grades weren't good enough to earn him a break on the insurance, which he had to pay himself. Finally he got a job. So now he drives to work to pay for insurance and gas and has no time or money to get into trouble. I like that arrangement.

My fourteen-year-old insists she should be able to drive by now. She gets to take Driver's Ed. next year but I can't decide if we should let her on the road. She can't find her shoes even when she's tripping over them. Yeah, I remember being a teenager and I'm scared stiff. I still have three more kids to go. I had always hoped the Millennium would be ushered in before I ever had teenagers but it's too late—I've already got them!

And yet, amidst all the confusion, there is joy in raising children. It comes when you sit in the audience as your child sings in his first concert, when one of them stands to "bury" their testimony, when they sink a basket with the flair of a Michael Jordan, when they come downstairs after taking half the afternoon getting ready for a dance, when they learn to count to a hundred, when they pray, when they wave at you from the stand when the Primary sings on Mother's Day, when you hear that voice over the phone, "Mom, I'm at Christopher's; can I stay?"

My children are becoming their own people now—for the most part. My seven-year-old thinks he should still be able to sit on my lap, which would be fine except that he's almost as tall as his mother! As I watch these people that are my children grow and develop, I'm glad to know that no matter how old they get, they will still need me for something. I know, because I learned what a "momma's girl" I was when I moved 750 miles away from Mom. Darwin finally moved us back to save on the phone bills! I was so shocked to find how much I missed my mom. I'd always thought it would be wonderful to be away from all her advice and meddling. Who'd have known I wasn't prepared to cut the apron strings! That's how I know my kids will still need me for something . . . no matter how old they get!

I'D LIKE A MOM TO GO PLEASE

AS A YOUNG MOTHER, WHEN MY CHILDREN WERE SMALL, I remember complaining to my mom that I never did anything except stay at home and take care of the kids. She smiled and assured me that "this, too, would pass."

"Wait 'till the kids get to be teenagers," she said. "You'll wish you had the time you have now."

I laughed her to scorn, then. Now that I have teenagers, I'm finding she was right. I spend every waking minute fulfilling the wants and desires of seven other people. I have three separate calenders just to record everything I need to do: a home calendar, a school calendar, and a church calendar. Trying to coordinate them is like performing a juggling act. If one gets misplaced, I'm lost. I know that on my computer there's a program that would help me get organized, but there's never a chance for me to get on the computer, except 4:00 a.m.—and I'm not thinking about time management then.

I'm one of the only moms at home in the afternoon on our block and there's always someone that needs to be taken somewhere. My life revolves around which sport is being offered during which season. My van is cluttered with shin guards, baseball mitts, basketball shorts and stinky old socks. Sometimes I even find petrified Happy Meals that not even the dog wants.

The kids love to see just how many people we can fit into our eight-passenger Caravan. I have gotten a basketball team, a dance team, and a scout troop in—but not usually at the same time. Fitting the entire Young Women's organization in at once is really pushing it. I know there are laws about overloading vehicles, but someone has to get those kids to their destinations!

The funny thing is that I hate to drive. It scares me! Driving around with all those kids is nerve wracking, and as a young mom, I refused to drive. Now if I don't drive, there's total chaos in the world.

It's a good thing that as times have changed and things have gotten so busy that the world had changed right along with it. I'm happy there's "drive through" everything. Not having to turn the car off or get out saves time and energy. Of course, now that my children are grown, I just send one of the bigger kids in if there's no drive-through facilities. That way, I'm ready to peel out as soon as they get back. I've got the reputation of being the "U-Turn Mom." It's become one of my greatest talents.

I used to hate eating in the car, but I've gotten over that. If I want to feed my kids, sometimes it's my only option. I've thought about making seventy-two hour kits just for the van but I haven't had the time. My kids keep telling me we need a bigger van.

I went on a trip with some friends and they had a van that had the WORKS. We were able to watch a video while lounging in comfort, our drinks being held so that nothing would get spilled—while the driver listened to the radio. My kids would love a van like that—but there's no way! I'd end up having to do all the driving because my family are vidiots!

With all the chasing around I do, the best thing that has ever happened to keep me organized is a cellular phone. I'm sure Idaho was one of the last states to offer cellular phone service, but now that we have it, there's no way to live without it. I can be going out of town and still call my kids and give them a list of things to get done before I get back. It's a little annoying to have to deal with arguments at home when you're on a date with your husband, but that's the price that must be paid for having the joy of being able to reach your kids from anywhere.

Cellulars are great. I've had a friend call me from her cellular, sitting out in my driveway, because she's been honking and I was doing something in the other end of the house and hadn't heard her. Now that's getting bad! But even cellular phones could never make me love having to play Taxi twenty-four hours a day.

As you already know, I hate to drive, but my husband loves to! I call him Mario Andretti. He loves to be behind the wheel and go fast! That triple decker bridge in Portland gave him a thrill, but it gave me a heart attack.

I think it's great that our oldest son doesn't like to drive on ice or in snow. He'll actually ask us to take him where he needs to go. (Of course that puts me back behind the wheel.) I've got a couple of other sons that have the speed demon look in their eyes, so I'm not looking forward to them getting a license.

Sometimes I can't wait until I have more drivers in the family, but it frightens me because then I have to worry about them behind the wheel. At least I should have more time. There are only so many hours in a day and people keep telling me that there are still twenty-four, but I've totally lost most of them to the car . Too bad being a Taxi Mom isn't tax deductible. I'd be a wealthy woman with all the miles I log every year. I saw a bumper sticker once that said: If I'm a housewife why do I spend my life in the car? That's exactly what I'd like to know, but I don't have time to ponder the question now. I just received another "to go" order.

CHIVALRY'S NOT DEAD — JUST CRIPPLED

I TRULY FEEL SORRY FOR MEN TODAY. They have got to be so confused. A hundred years ago a man was a man and a woman was a woman, no questions asked. Today? Well, here's what society thinks:

A MAN SHOULD BE

1.   Strong: Physically, mentally, emotionally; with degrees in all three so that he can make informed decisions about anything in any of those categories at any given time.

2.   Sensitive: Constantly aware of his mates' needs and desires and even able to understand why she has certain needs and desires.

3.   Caring: It goes with sensitive because if he's aware of his mate's needs he clearly knows she wants him to take care of her—no wait—care about her. (She can take care of herself.)

4.   Sure of himself: He's so sure he can even cry if necessary; it's acceptable now.

5.   Mr. Mom: A man should want to nurture and bond with his children as much as a woman does—and even change diapers. (This varies, even among LDS men. Some do, some don't change diapers. Thank goodness mine would.)

Okay, now let's add the gospel requirements:

A MAN SHOULD:

1. Uphold his priesthood when he's too tired to even hold up his head.

2. Fulfill his callings and support his spouse in her callings, often spending date night at a correlation meeting together.

3. Be the patriarch in the home even though most of his family is scattered over half the town most of the time.

4. Be a loving father to his offspring which often consists of kissing them hello and goodnight at the same time.

Add all these together and "TaDa," you've got millions of overwhelmed men!

Just as we strive to be Molly, they are striving to become "Marvin Mormon," perfect mate for Molly. It can't be any easier for them that it is for us. I bet they're so thankful they have only one wife. Can you imagine trying to please several '90s women? Scary, huh?

When Heavenly Father put my husband together he certainly had me in mind. We are exactly right for each other. Having both been married before, we have a sure testimony that this is true. So even with our respective faults, we are grateful for each other. We are a perfect match.

He's Mr. Procrastination.
I'm Get-it-done Sally

He's the epitome of patience.
I'm certain that patience is a character flaw, though I've heard it is a virtue. I don't have time to find out for sure.

He's soft spoken and tactful.
I'm constantly waiting for my brain to catch up with my mouth.

He's shy.
I'm not, and don't even know the meaning of the word.

He's tall and slender.
I'm pleasantly plump.

He sews.
I don't.

But with all our differences, we have the same beliefs and the same desire to live the gospel. We also share a love of basketball. He plays, I watch—none too quietly.

The question remains: "Is Marvin Mormon ready to head into the next century? I feel that any man who is really trying to live the gospel and be true to his covenants is automatically ready for the next millennium. I also think that a man devoid of offense toward God and man is automatically sure of himself. . . and that tears are a gift of the Spirit. And if he's living the Word of Wisdom and treating his body like a temple, he'll have all the strength we'll ever want. Is my husband ready for 2000? Yes, I believe he is. We have a 50/50 arrangement—half the time! He's bigger than me and I feel really safe. He cares for me and is very sensitive—unless there's something good on TV. He's very sure of himself—unless my mom is mad. (She grows ten feet taller when she's angry.) He will help me with the kids, though he never kept it a secret that he was glad I nursed all the babies and saved him from those 2 A.M. feedings.

In our relationship, chivalry is not dead. Darwin is a great example of what a true gentleman should be. He opens the car door for me and helps me out—unless we're both preoccupied with toddlers refusing to sit in their car seats and older kids fighting for the window. Sometimes my sons even open the door for me now. That's encouraging. Hopefully they'll continue the habit. With men like my husband teaching their sons how to treat a lady, I know chivalry will never die. It might be severely wounded, but I have faith the next generation will at least keep it hobbling along on crutches!

WE STOPPED READING OUR SCRIPTURES TOGETHER TO SAVE OUR MARRIAGE

I WAS RAISED IN THE CHURCH BUT TRAVELLED FOR A FEW YEARS THROUGH THE MISTS OF DARKNESS (see 1 Nephi 8, 11). Then, at the age of twenty-four, I gained a burning testimony. Some people have said I'm a gospel fanatic now, but it's not fanaticism, it's deep love and gratitude to the Savior for atoning for me. When I finally found my husband, we were both wounded and weary from failed marriages and the ravages of this old world. We vowed we'd end each day with scripture study and prayer. We tried. We really did, but with children to tuck in and get drinks for and turn the light on in the bathroom for, scripture study became a chore.

Darwin would start, reading his allotted number of verses out loud. I would then start mine and within two sentences he'd be out like a light! I would be furious. How could he fall asleep so fast—and right in the middle of Nephi's return to Jerusalem for the Brass Plates! It became a source of contention in our newly married bliss. After about a month we compromised. We'd study the scriptures independently and then discuss them at breakfast or in the car—anywhere other than bed. It's worked out a lot better because he stays awake during our discussions. Of course, I insist on reading to the children in the morning and they don't have a choice. If they want to eat, they listen, with their eyes open. It took us a year to complete the Book of Mormon, but we did it! Sometimes I wondered if it was worth it until my toddler wanted to know where the "skiptures" were if we forgot.

As a Latter-day Saint woman, I realize that my personal spiritual growth is my own responsibility. No one can do it for me though I take my children's growth into my own hands. They are happy just puttering around and I can only let them do that part of the time. My husband—well, he must work out his own salvation with fear and sleeping—oops—I mean trembling. (Mormon 9:27)

I'm actually amazed how much of the gospel he gets through osmosis. I'll be sitting in sacrament meeting trying to keep my kids from ripping the scriptures to shred as they fight, and I look over at my husband and he's sleeping! I'm living for the day when I can sit through a meeting with all my jewelry in place, my dress still neatly pressed, and my hair in the same style I started with, and my husband is sleeping! It amazes me that he could fall asleep so easily, because we have sacrament meeting first thing in the morning. Granted, he has two early morning meetings, but I get up just as early to get all the kids ready, and I stay awake! Maybe the Spirit lulls him into a place no woman can go.

At this time in our lives he's Ward Mission Leader, so I get to sit with him in Sacrament Meeting, but he already know if he's ever called to be in the bishopric the entire family will sit in the front row armed with pea shooters, ready to help him stay awake. The boys are looking forward to it!

His memory is a mystery to me, too. I've talked to many women in the Church who tell me their righteous man can't remember anything, either. It is an utter shock to my husband that Monday night is Family Home Evening, even though it's been that way all our lives.

I've just come to the conclusion that men need to be reminded about everything from family prayer to brushing their teeth. I guess we'd all be happier if we just accepted it and got on with life. Men are so busy trying to support a family, magnify their priesthood, keep up with today's pace and wade through the confusion of the "'90s Kinda Guy Syndrome," that it wouldn't hurt us women to try and help them remember little things like prayer and teeth.

My husband and I have a deal. I remind him of all the things he's too busy to remember and when he's standing before a large audience he thanks his "lovely wife" for all her support. Just in case he forgets, I sign all my letters and cards: "Love, Your Lovely Wife, Kim." It's become a funny reminder and he does remember. I tease him a lot, but I am truly thankful for his loving care of our family. It's a joy to have a companion that has the same goals as I do.

As I ponder my life as it is now, I am comforted by what I see. There are many things I don't do that might help me earn my Molly Mormon Certificate, but there are many things I DO that keep me on the path. I've become content with that. My family isn't suffering, I hope, and every now and then, they all catch a glimpse of what I'm trying to teach them.

Now, when I think of Molly and her perfection, I'm not such a basket case. After all, we are put on this earth to learn to become like Heavenly Father, not Molly. Study of the gospel has taught me that this process will extend far beyond this existence. We've got eons to get perfected! I think Father is proud of us for giving it the old college try each day. That knowledge combined with, "I'd like to "bury" my testimony," "But Mawm! Pink does go with green, see" and "You're so pretty, Mom, even if you are a little fat," make being a Mormon wife and mother worth the struggle. I may never get that certificate on my wall, but I do have quite collection of pictures, finger prints, and elementary art work done in indelible ink. Is there any better tribute to the Myth? I may not be 100% Molly, but she's not 100% without me!

ABOUT THE AUTHOR

Kimberly Olsen was born in Fort Wayne, Indiana quite a few years ago (less than 40). She moved to Idaho with her family in her youth where she has lived since. (Except for those happy years in Portland, Oregon) She is the lovely wife of Darwin Sr. and they are the parents of a combined family of six kids. She has received her degree from The School of Hard Knocks with a Ph.D. in Trials and Tribulation. This is her first published book with more to soon follow! She has worked in Primary, Young Women, and has led ward choirs. Presently, she and Darwin are serving a stake mission in the Blackfoot Idaho South Stake

ABOUT THE ILLUSTRATOR

Dustin Baird was barely out of preschool when it became obvious to everyone that he had enormous talent and creativity. He quickly became proficient with the use of pencil, paint, brush, and clay. He was just twelve years old when he was offered his first teaching position at a local art academy. At fourteen he designed the company logo for a large auto dealership. At the ripe old age of sixteen, Dustin finds himself in high demand as a cartoonist and illustrator. He is currently living and teaching art in Kaysville, Utah.